I CAN MAKE GOD GLAD!

Mary E. Erickson

With Illustrations by Len Ebert

Chariot Books™
A Division of Cook Communications

To my SCBWI critique group in Colorado Springs:
Carol Reinsma, Beverly Lewis, Vicki Fox, Peggy Marshall

They have contributed greatly to my three picture books
on the attributes of God.

Chariot Books™ is an imprint of Chariot Family Publishing.
Cook Communications Ministries, Elgin, Illinois 60120
Cook Communications Ministries, Paris, Ontario
Kingsway Communications, Eastbourne, England

I CAN MAKE GOD GLAD!
© 1995 by Mary E. Erickson

Scripture quotations are from the *Holy Bible, New International Version,* © 1973, 1978, 1984, International Bible Society. Used by permission of Zondervan Bible Publishers.

Cover and interior design by Paetzold Design
Cover illustration by Len Ebert
First Printing, 1994
Printed in Singapore
99 98 97 96 95   5 4 3 2 1

Library of Congress Cataloging-in-Publication Data

Erickson, Mary E.
I can make God glad! / Mary Erickson.
p. cm.
ISBN 0-7814-0102-X
1. Children—Religious life. 2. Children—Conduct of life. [1. Conduct of life. 2. Christian life. 3. Prayer books and devotions.] I. Title.
BV4571.2.E75   1994
248.8'2—dc20
93-33070
CIP
AC

The children in Miss Cathy's Sunday school class sang:

> *"Jesus loves me! this I know,*
> *for the Bible tells me so.*
> *Little ones to Him belong.*
> *They are weak, but He is strong.*
>
> *Yes, Jesus loves me.*
> *Yes, Jesus loves me.*
> *Yes, Jesus loves me.*
> *The Bible tells me so.*
>
> *Jesus loves me when I'm good,*
> *when I do the things I should.*
> *Jesus loves me when I'm bad,*
> *but it makes Him very sad."*

Jeff wiggled on his red chair. "I don't want to make God sad. I want to make Him glad."

Miss Cathy said, "Let's talk about that."

And they did.

In this book you'll read stories like those Miss Cathy told her class.

Perhaps they will help you understand how you can make God glad too.

Praising God

KOREA

"Today is Chusok!" said Ok Chi. "It's picnic time."

Her sister, Mee Yung, said, "I'm going to wear my long blue dress to visit Grandpa's grave. It was his favorite."

When the Pak family reached the cemetery, people were already celebrating the Korean festival of Chusok.

Ok Chi asked, "Why are they putting food on the graves?"

"It's an offering," explained Father. "They're giving thanks for the good harvest."

"But we don't do that," Mee Yung said.

"No, because we worship God. We thank Him, not our dead relatives."

Mother unpacked the dried fish, apples, and rice snug inside its seaweed wrapper.

"Let's make up a prayer," Ok Chi said, "and sing it out loud."

Bowing her head, she sang softly, "Dear God, You are wise. You are good. You send the sun and rain that make the rice and apples grow."

Mee Yung sang, "Thanks for the mountain flowers that brighten Grandpa's grave."

Father's voice was deep. "We love You, Lord Jesus."

Mother added, "And praise Your wonderful name."

Together the family sang, "Amen."

Dear God,
When I talk about how great You are, I think that makes You feel good.
I'm going to try to praise You every day.

Doing Good

AND DO NOT FORGET TO DO GOOD AND TO SHARE WITH OTHERS,
FOR WITH SUCH SACRIFICES GOD IS PLEASED. HEBREWS 13:16

The Cruz family raised pigs. Every day Joel helped his sister and brother carry water to the pigs and feed them corn.

Sometimes the family roasted a pig on a holiday, but usually they sold the pigs to earn money for food and clothes.

Father had given Joel his very own pig. Every week when Joel gave Figgy a bath, he said, "Figgy, you are the most beautiful pig in the Philippines."

One night a typhoon hit their village. The family prayed and huddled together all night. In the morning their neighbor's house was gone.

Father said, "I'm going to cut down bamboo trees for their new home."

"I can drag in palm fronds for the roof," said Panfilo.

Erlinda said, "I'll give a dress to Caren."

"I'll cook some rice," said Mother.

What can I do? thought Joel. Just then Figgy ran between his legs. Joel grabbed her by the tail and carried her to the neighbors.

"Here's Figgy," he said. "But you mustn't eat her. When she becomes a mother, you can sell her piglets."

Thank You, God, for my home and food. Many people are hungry or homeless.
Show me how I can help them.

Working Willingly

BOLIVIA

In Bolivia lived a farmer and his family. Their mud brick house was small. Their meals were simple.

"Who will scrub potatoes for dinner?" Mother asked.

"I'm tired of scrubbing potatoes," complained the oldest daughter. "I'm also tired of eating them."

"I'll help," said Elena. Humming softly, the six year old scrubbed potatoes and peeled onions for stew.

After dinner, Mother asked her son to get water.

"I always have to fetch the water," he grumbled, grabbing a bucket.

The next morning Father asked, "Who will help me tend the sheep today?"

"It's too windy," said the oldest daughter.

"My feet are sore," complained the son.

"I'll go," said Elena.

Father and Elena led the sheep to a grassy plain. All day she watched the sheep so they wouldn't wander away.

That night Father tucked the patch quilt under Elena's chin and kissed her forehead. "You may be small," he said, "but you're a cheerful helper. You made me happy today."

Dear God,
Children in Bolivia have chores. So do I. Help me not to complain.
I want to be a cheerful helper too.

Obeying Parents

CHILDREN, OBEY YOUR PARENTS IN EVERYTHING, FOR THIS PLEASES THE LORD.
COLOSSIANS 3:20

Two brothers rode their bicycles down the hill.

"Ah-h!" said Mark. "I love the wind in my face. I can hardly wait to ride in the mountains Saturday."

"Me either," Josh said.

"It's time for supper," said Mark. "Let's cut through the alley behind the junkyard."

"Dad said not to ride through there."

"That's a silly rule! Besides, he'll never know. Come on."

"Not me," Josh said.

"Fraidy cat!" shouted Mark, turning into the alley. "I'll beat you home."

On Saturday morning, Dad called, "Hey, guys, ready for our bike ride?"

In the garage, Mark groaned. "My tire is flat."

Dad pulled a sharp piece of steel out of the tire. "Where'd this come from?"

"In the alley behind the junkyard," Mark mumbled.

Josh asked, "Can you fix it, Dad?"

"It's beyond repair. Mark will need a new tire."

"I guess I'll miss the bike ride. It's my own fault."

Mark's heart felt as flat as his tire as he watched two bikes head for the mountain trail.

Dear God,
Please help me obey my parents. I feel bad when I don't.
I feel good when I do. And I know it's best for me.

Being Friendly

THE ALIEN LIVING WITH YOU MUST BE TREATED AS ONE OF YOUR NATIVE-BORN.
LOVE HIM AS YOURSELF. LEVITICUS 19:34

Somboon glanced at the boy huddled in the corner of the bamboo schoolroom. His ragged shirt was clean. His feet were bare. His eyes were wide with fear.

"We have a new third grader," said the teacher. "Ho Minh moved to Thailand from Vietnam. He understands a few Thai words. Who will share his desk and books with Minh?"

Somboon scooted across his bench. He led Minh back to his double desk.

Opening his reader, Somboon pointed to pictures and whispered, "School. Teachers. Girls. Boys. Ball."

Minh stared at the words.

Somboon felt Minh's leg shaking. He pointed to himself and said, "Friend."

During recess the boys played soccer. Someone kicked the ball to Minh. He trapped it with his bare foot. Quick as a kick boxer, he dribbled the ball in and out among the boys. He kicked it past the goalie and into the net.

His team cheered.

Slapping him on the back, Somboon said, "Good kick!"

Minh smiled. "Good school!" he said. "You . . . good friend."

Dear God,
It's scary being the new kid. When people move to my city,
help me think of ways to be friendly and kind.

Telling the Truth

Lori laid the flowers on the kitchen table. "I picked the prettiest ones for Mother's birthday bouquet."

"You sure did." Granny smiled. "Here's a white vase you can use. I'm going out to weed my garden."

That vase isn't special enough, Lori thought. *I'll use Granny's blue vase from Japan.* Lori climbed onto the cabinet counter. Stretching on tiptoe, she reached the top shelf. *Crash!*

"Oh, no!" gasped Lori. "What will I tell Granny?"

Lori swept up the pieces of blue glass. Quickly she hid them in the trash. After arranging the flowers in the white vase, she went outside.

"How do the flowers look?" asked Granny, leaning on her hoe.

"Pretty."

"Then why do you look so sad?"

Bending over, Lori tugged on a weed. A voice inside whispered, *Don't tell the truth. Tell her you've got a headache.*

"I . . . I have . . . a . . . Oh, Granny, I broke your blue vase!" Lori sobbed.

"I feel sad about the vase." Granny patted Lori's head. "But thank you for being brave enough to tell me what happened."

Dear God,
Sometimes it's hard to tell the truth and so easy to tell a lie.
Make me strong so I'll always tell the truth.

Taking Care of My Body

DO YOU NOT KNOW THAT YOUR BODY IS A TEMPLE OF THE HOLY SPIRIT?
I CORINTHIANS 6:19

Benito stuffed the third doughnut into his mouth. *"Hasta luego, Madre,"* he called, running to catch the school bus.

At recess Jose said, "Hey, Benito, want some candy? I broke the piñata at a party last night."

Benito ate two chocolate bars. Later Sara gave him some cheesy chips.

During math Benito's stomach was turning flip-flops. At the nurse's office he threw up; then he lay down on a cot to rest.

Suddenly the door flew open. In came a teacher, helping a big kid who could hardly walk.

"Call 911!" shouted the teacher.

I wonder what's wrong, thought Benito. *I can't see any blood, and he isn't crying.*

Minutes later paramedics carried the sleeping boy out on a stretcher.

"What happened?" Benito asked the nurse.

"He swallowed pills someone gave him on the playground. At the hospital, a doctor will pump the drugs out of his stomach."

Benito looked at the poster on the wall. "Just say NO to drugs," it read.

He rubbed his sore stomach. *I'd better say NO to junk food today,* he thought. *I may need to say NO to drugs mañana.*

Dear God,
Help me make wise choices. I want to stay healthy
and strong because my body belongs to You.

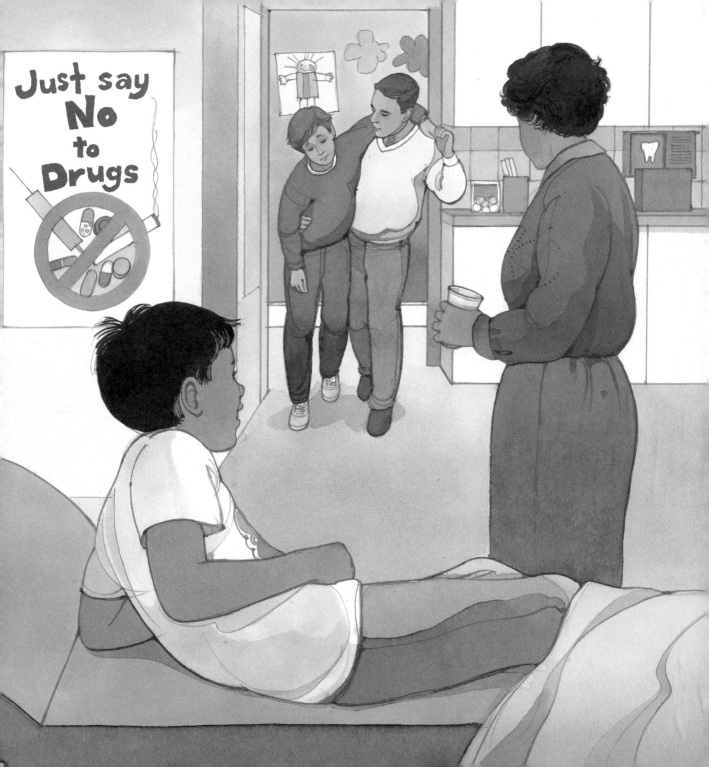

Forgiving Each Other

BE KIND AND COMPASSIONATE TO ONE ANOTHER, FORGIVING EACH OTHER,
JUST AS IN CHRIST GOD FORGAVE YOU. EPHESIANS 4:32

The warm waves washed over their feet as Tahani and Abby walked along the Hawaiian beach.

"I think we have enough," said Tahani, putting a fan-shaped shell into her bucket.

The girls dumped their shells onto the beach. Patting and molding wet sand, they each built a castle. They made walls around them with the shells. Later, they danced around their castles.

Tahani sang, "We are princesses of Hawaii."

Abby sang, "We'll marry the sons of the king."

Together they sang, "And live happily ever af—"

Suddenly Abby slipped, smashing Tahani's castle.

"Look what you've done!" shouted Tahani.

Abby sobbed, "Don't be mad. I didn't mean to."

"Yes, you did!" said Tahani. And she left.

When Tahani returned, her castle had been rebuilt. Abby was gone. But printed in the sand were these words: "I'M SORRY."

Tahani found Abby under a palm tree.

"I'm sorry I got mad," said Tahani. "Let's forgive each other and be friends."

Hand in hand, the girls ran laughing and splashing into the waves.

Dear God,
I'm glad You forgive me when I do wrong.
Help me to forgive others with love, just as You forgive me.

Sharing with Others

DO TO OTHERS AS YOU WOULD HAVE THEM DO TO YOU. LUKE 6:31

"Look! I caught one!" said Rufino, holding up a green turtle. "I'll name him Gorkis the Great of the Dominican Republic."

Carlos splashed down the creek. He saw a spotted turtle sunning on a rock. When he tried to grab it, the turtle slid into the water.

"Help me catch one," pleaded Carlos.

"Can't! Gotta go. Gotta fix a new home for Gorkis."

In Rufino's backyard, the boys found a battered washtub. They put three large rocks in the bottom. Then they filled the tub with water.

"Can I hold him?" Carlos asked.

"Catch your own pet." Rufino put the turtle in the tub.

Carlos's smile disappeared like the sun on a cloudy day.

"What's wrong?" Rufino asked.

Shoving his hands into his pockets, Carlos trudged away.

Rufino thought. *What if he had caught this turtle? What if he had told me I couldn't touch it? How would I feel?*

"Carlos, come back!" he called. "You can hold *our* turtle. We'll fix another tub at your house. Then you can take Gorkis home every other night."

The boys rubbed the turtle's slippery back. They laughed when Gorkis pushed his head out and nipped their fingertips.

Dear God,
Friends are special. Help me to treat them the way I want to be treated.

Helping Each Other

UGANDA

CARRY EACH OTHER'S BURDENS, AND IN THIS WAY YOU WILL
FULFILL THE LAW OF CHRIST. GALATIANS 6:2

Another school day was over in Uganda. Nankya and her best friend walked outside together.

"Stay and play stones," begged her friend.

"I wish I could," said Nankya, "but I have an important job to do."

Nankya hurried down the path through the banana trees. When she reached home, her aunt was waiting in the doorway. She looked tired. *No wonder,* thought Nankya. *She has seven children to care for.*

Her aunt said, "I'm so glad you're here. The baby has been fussing all day."

Nankya picked up her crying cousin. "Nanky is here," she said. With a cool, wet cloth she wiped away the tears running down the baby's chubby cheeks.

Her aunt sat down at the treadle sewing machine. "I must finish these school uniforms tonight." She sighed. "I couldn't do my job, Nankya, if you didn't carry the water and play with the children each night."

"Sometimes in the night I remember Mama and Papa," said Nankya. "When they died, my brothers and I were scared and lonely." Nankya kissed her aunt's cheek. "We wouldn't have a home without you, Auntie."

Dear God,
Thank You for people who love and care for me.
When someone needs me, I can be a helper too.

Praying for Others

I URGE THAT PRAYERS AND THANKSGIVING BE MADE FOR EVERYONE. THIS IS GOOD, AND PLEASES GOD. I TIMOTHY 2:1, 3

Winds whistled down a frozen canal in Holland. Sitting on a tree stump, Lucas laced up his skating boots.

When the race began, a dozen skates scraped the ice.

Soon Lucas was in the lead. But right behind him came big Hugo, swinging his arms wildly. As Hugo skated past, he laughed and hit Lucas in the face.

Near the finish line, Lucas caught up with Hugo. Stretching his leg, Hugo bumped Lucas's skate.

Thump!

Lucas fell, sliding across the canal.

At supper Father asked, "What's wrong, Lucas?"

"I was last in the race today," Lucas mumbled.

"You're a good skater," Father said. "What happened?"

"Hugo made me fall."

Mother asked, "Isn't he the boy who doesn't have a father?"

"Yes. And his mother works two jobs."

Father picked up the newspaper. "Some boys do strange things to get attention."

In his bed, Lucas talked to God. "Please help Hugo not to be mean. Maybe he's lonely for his father. This is hard to say, Lord, but . . . if You help me, I'll try to be his friend."

Dear God,
Praying for my family is easy. I know You want me to pray for others, too,
like my teacher, our president, and kids who act mean.

Giving Cheerfully

PERÚ

Fredy whistled as he ran down the dirt path to his bamboo home in Lima, Peru. His mother was hanging out the laundry.

"Look what I got from America!" shouted Fredy, waving a birthday card. "The note says, 'Buy something special with this money.' "

"Like what?" his mother asked.

"Oh, maybe a soccer ball or a painting set." Fredy smiled. "Or a book filled with pictures of wild animals."

On Sunday morning Fredy sat on the church bench beside his father.

The pastor said, "We're going to take an offering for Mrs. Fernandez. If she can't pay her rent tomorrow, she and her children will sleep in the street."

We're poor too, Fredy thought. *But I have a father. And a home. And a friend in America.* He felt the money in his pocket.

When the offering basket came by, Fredy dropped in some of his birthday money.

Next the children's band played. Fredy blew softly across the hollow bamboo stalks of his zampoña.

He sang the words in his head: "I have the joy, joy, joy, joy down in my heart."

I really do! he thought.

Dear God,
You have given me so much. When I give my offering to You,
I want to do it joyfully.

Doing What's Fair

UNITED STATES

GOD IS PLEASED WHEN WE ARE JUST AND FAIR.
PROVERBS 21:3 (TLB)

Kris pushed Becky's wheelchair across the patio.

"My legs are getting stronger," said Becky. "Soon I'll be walking again."

Becky's mother brought out a snack. "The doctor said swimming is good exercise. But Becky can't do it alone."

"I'm glad I can help," said Kris, dunking a chocolate chip cookie into her milk. "I'll be back next week."

Next Saturday Kris was stuffing her suit into her gym bag when the phone rang.

"Hi!" It was Jenny, her best friend. "Mom said she'll take us skating and then to McDonald's. Can you come?"

"Wish I could," said Kris, "but I promised Becky I'd—"

"That's not fair," Jenny whined. "I thought *I* was your best friend."

"I have to be fair to Becky, too. She's counting on me."

"Well!" Jenny sounded mad. "It's your decision."

"I'll see you Monday." Slowly Kris hung up the phone.

Later, in the pool, Becky and Kris pretended to be dolphins. They kicked and leaped and giggled and splashed.

This is fun, thought Kris. *And I feel good inside.*

Dear God,
Being fair isn't always easy. Help me do the right thing in school,
on the playground, and at home.

Loving Jesus

RUSSIA

IF ANYONE LOVES ME, HE WILL OBEY MY TEACHING.
MY FATHER WILL LOVE HIM. JOHN 14:23

Ivan squirmed on his chair in the old stone church in Moscow. "I thought we didn't believe in God," he said.

"Things have changed in Russia," the teacher answered. "Now everyone can go to Sunday school and learn about God." She sat down and opened a Bible storybook.

Ivan pointed to a picture of a man in a purple robe with a thorny crown on his head. "Who's that?" he asked.

"It's Jesus," said the teacher.

As she read the Easter story, Ivan listened to every word. He brushed away a tear when he saw Jesus on the cross.

"He died for me?" Ivan couldn't believe it. "But I was against God."

"He died to forgive all of us. Jesus can make us right with God," said the teacher.

"What do I have to do?" asked Ivan.

"You must ask Him to come into your heart."

"I'd like to do that," said Ivan.

"Me too," said Boris.

That day two Russian boys knelt and invited Jesus to live in their hearts.

Into my heart, Into my heart,
Come into my heart, Lord Jesus.
Come in today. Come in to stay.
Come into my heart, Lord Jesus.

Now if you obey me fully ...
You will be my treasured possession.

Exodus 19:5